Antony Kamm

SCOTTIES SERIES EDITORS
Frances and Gordon Jarvie

Contents

Raiders 2–6	Pirate doctors 32–34
Hijackers and mutineers 7–10	Ballads and books 35–37
Kidnappers 11–13	Pirate punishment 38
Privateers or pirates? 14–20	Modern piracy 39
Patriot or pirate? 21	Answers, places of interest, and a pirate map of Scotland 40
Scottish pirates of the Golden Age 22–28	Facts and activities .... i–viii
Pirate hunters 29–31	

Published in 2019 by
NMS Enterprises Limited – Publishing
a division of NMS Enterprises Limited
National Museums Scotland
Chambers Street, Edinburgh EH1 1JF

Text © The Estate of Antony Kamm 2019.
Images (for ©, see below and page viii of 'Facts and activities' section).

ISBN: 978-1-910682-03-6

No part of this publication may be reproduced, stored in a retrieval system or transmitted, in any form or by any means, electronic, mechanical, photocopying, recording or otherwise, without prior permission of the publisher.

The right of Antony Kamm to be identified as the author of this book has been asserted by him in accordance with the Copyright, Designs and Patents Act 1988.

British Library Cataloguing in Publication Data
A catalogue record of this book
is available from the British Library.

Book design concept by Redpath.
Cover design by Mark Blackadder.
Layout by NMS Enterprises Ltd – Publishing.
Printed and bound in the United Kingdom by Henry Ling Limited, Dorchester, Dorset.

CREDITS

Thanks are due to all individuals and organisations who have supplied images for this publication. Every attempt has been made to contact relevant copyright holders. If any image has been inadvertently missed, please contact the publisher.

© NATIONAL MUSEUMS SCOTLAND
Cover (Wood's victory), p. 2 (Mackinnon Cross; viking ship, model); p. 3 (cast seal, Alexander III); p. 4 (*Mary Willoughby*, model); p. 5 (Elizabeth I ship, model); p. 6 (map); p. 12 (Falkland Palace); p. 13 (seal, Joan Beaufort); p. 15 (*Yellow Carvel*, model; Margaret Tudor); p. 16 (window, James VI); p. 17 (sea-chest); p. 21 (watch); p. 22 (flint-lock pistol); p. 26 (Cape Coast Castle); p. 27 (sword); p. 28 (thumbscrews); p. 33 (Leith Harbour); p. 37 (Captain Hook); p. 40 (lantern; octant); throughout (seascape); Activities section – p. ii (pirate montage).

FURTHER CREDITS
(see page viii of 'Facts and activities' section)

For a full listing of NMS Enterprises
Limited – Publishing titles and related merchandise:

www.nms.ac.uk/books

Raiders

How some invaders from over the seas returned to stay in Scotland; and how early Scottish pirates plundered the ships, lands and property of others.

The Roman historian **Ammianus Marcellinus**, writing of the year AD 360, describes marauding Irish warriors causing havoc in the north. They were from the tribe of Dál Riata and had come to join the Picts in harassing the Roman overlords of the province of Britain.

The Picts were the hereditary occupiers of what is now central and northern Scotland. The Dál Riata, whom the Romans called *Scotti* or Scots, subsequently raided Pictish lands, settling in about AD 450 in the region of Argyll.

Two separate peoples, **Picts** and **Scots**, each with their own territory, became three at the end of the 8th century when the **Vikings** in their longships began to arrive in 795 from Scandinavia. They came first as pirates, then as settlers, occupying the Western Isles, Orkney, Shetland – even areas of the northern and western mainland.

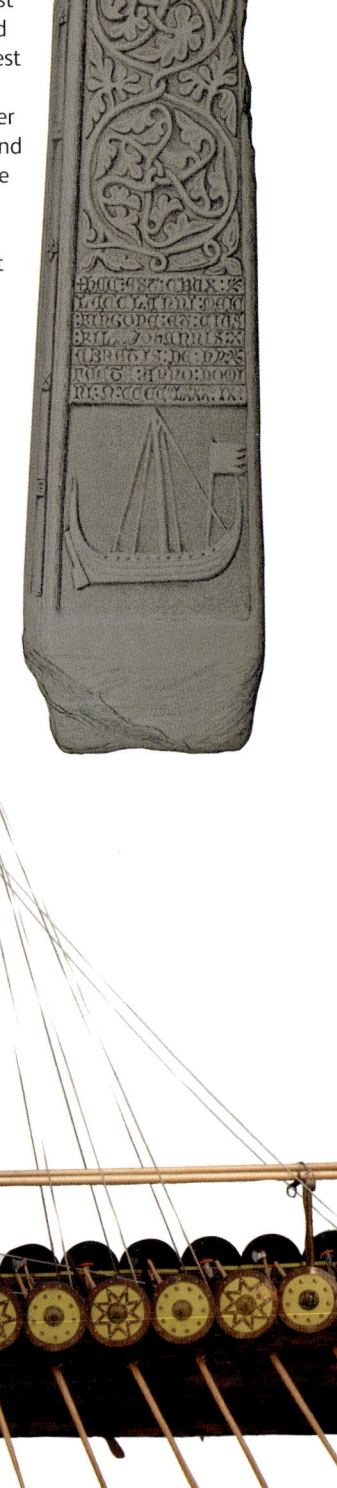

Right: This lower section of a cross fragment from Iona, off the western coast of Scotland, is dated 1489. It shows a West Highland galley or *birlinn*, with a banner flying at the prow and a large rudder at the stern. Stern rudders were a key technological development of the earlier Norse longships (**below**), from which *birlinns* evolved.

It was the raiders, not the resident Picts, who finally prevailed. In 843 Kenneth MacAlpin, ruler of the Dál Riata, also became king of the Picts. Their combined territory became known as Scotia. The kingdom of Scotland was created in 1018 by Malcolm II, who took over the regions of Strathclyde and Lothian. Uneasy relations continued, however, with the Vikings, whose hold on Scottish territory lasted until 1469 when Orkney and Shetland were surrendered to King James III on his marriage to the Danish princess Margaret.

The Vikings sold the Isle of Man, along with the Western Isles, to King Alexander III of Scotland in 1266. But by the beginning of the 16th century, the Isle of Man was under the control of England. In 1507 the Lord of Man, **Thomas Stanley, 2nd Earl of Derby**, attacked Galloway in south-west Scotland with such ferocity that the town of Kirkcudbright was almost destroyed.

Above: A carrack is a three- or four-masted ship that was used in 14th–15th century Europe. This one, from 1468, was part of the Scots Navy under King James III of Scotland.

Sir Alexander McCulloch of Whithorn, south-west of Kirkcudbright, took revenge on the Earl of Derby's actions. He manned a small fleet with his retainers (servants), sailed to Man, and carried off everything that was '*not too hot or heavy*' to be removed. And he returned, so often and without warning, that the Manx people, it is said, used to eat their meat before their soup to be sure of having something substantial in their stomachs before he arrived. They even had a prayer: '*Keep me, my good corn, and my sheep and bullocks / From Satan, from Sin, and those thievish McCullochs.*'

Above: Cast of the 2nd Great Seal of Alexander III, c.1265.

Left: A model of the Gokstad Viking ship, c.860. Built of overlapping planks, it could be propelled by 16 pairs of oars or by sail, and steered with an oar-shaped rudder.

3

In 1532, **Alexander**, Clan Chief of the Macdonalds, and **Hector Maclean of Duart** attacked the Isle of Man and captured an English ship, which was presented to King James V of Scotland.

Yet only a few years later, in 1535, the Crown made Alexander an outlaw for piracy against the ships of a Glasgow merchant off the Mull of Kintyre.

Capturing the king's ship

James V's Royal Scots Navy included a number of captured ships. The model above is of the English ship *Mary Willoughby*. Originally part of Henry VIII of England's fleet, it was named after Maria de Salinas (Countess Willoughby de Eresby), maid-of-honour to the king's first wife, Catherine of Aragon. Captured by the Scots in c.1533, these sails show the ship under Scottish ownership.

Ailean nan Sop (Allan of the Straws) got his name from his habit of lighting wisps of straw to set fire to buildings in the regions that he terrorised.

With a fleet of war galleys at his command, Allan would plunder, and often take over, districts that took his fancy or whose owners had offended him. Chiefs whom he did not kill were grateful enough to give him lands and castles, which became further bases for his operations in Ireland, the Western Isles, western Highlands, and even the Lowlands. Allan was a dangerous enemy, but a good friend to those who gave him favours, even including the Crown.

At the age of fifty, Allan retired from piracy, much to the disappointment of his followers. One day, at dinner in Tarbert, his castle on the Isle of Gigha, a guest remarked loudly that there was very little meat on the rib of beef he was picking over, observing, *'What a change has come over this house, when the bones are so bare!'* Allan was furious and ordered his men to *'make every ship ready to sail tonight and we shall try to get a little meat for the winter'*. They sailed up the Clyde to Erskine Ferry, near Renfrew, landed, and stole a vast number of cattle to bring back to Gigha. The expedition became known as the 'Foray of the Rib', after the original bone of contention.

Allan died peacefully in 1551 and was buried among his ancestors on the Isle of Iona.

Ruari MacNeil of Barra, 35th Chief of Clan MacNeil, was known as **Rory the Turbulent** – and for good reason.

Ruari, who lived at the end of the 16th century, kept a galley in a permanent state of readiness on the beach below Kisimul Castle, on the island of Barra in the Outer Hebrides, with a crew billeted in a nearby hut. Any ship, from whatever country, which passed within range of Kisimul was fair game to the MacNeil chief.

After a particularly successful foray against an English ship, Elizabeth I of England made a formal complaint about Ruari's piracy to James VI of Scotland. Having several reasons to please her, James ordered Ruari to appear before him in Edinburgh to explain himself. But he took no notice. James sent **Mackenzie of Kintail**, who seems to have been a bit of a rogue himself, to fetch MacNeil.

Mackenzie anchored his ship below Kisimul Castle and invited Ruari and his men to dine with him. He then plied them with so much drink that it was easy to clasp them in chains. Ruari was shipped off to Edinburgh to face the king.

A model of a galleon, fully-rigged, from the time of Queen Elizabeth I (1533–1603).

But Ruari was resourceful. When James reprimanded him for annoying Elizabeth, he replied that he only did it to seek revenge against the woman who 'killed your Majesty's mother' – a reference to Mary, Queen of Scots, executed in 1587 for her involvement in a conspiracy to assassinate Elizabeth. Although persuaded by Ruari's plea, James confiscated his estates in favour of the wily Mackenzie – who promptly rented them back to Ruari for an annual sum.

Kisimul Castle

It is said that after dining at Kisimul, Ruari would despatch a trumpeter to the battlements, with a herald who proclaimed, '*Hear, people, take heed, all you nations, the great MacNeil of Barra has finished his meal, and the princes of the world may now eat*'.

Folk in the western Highlands in the 16th century were a tough lot, but none tougher than **Neil MacLeod**.

King James VI set out to civilise the island of Lewis in the Outer Hebrides by setting up a co-operative of gentlemen from Fife (the '**Fife Adventurers**'), to establish a fishing colony at Stornoway. They faced much opposition from the locals, notably Neil, who had assumed control of the island.

His brother Murdoch captured a leading member of the Adventurers, but then fell out with Neil, who handed him over to justice. Murdoch was hanged at St Andrews, Fife, in 1599.

When Neil MacLeod seized Stornoway Castle from the Adventurers in 1605, the king again called on **Mackenzie of Kintail** (see page 5) to recapture the castle and to assist the settlers with a ship loaded with supplies. Instead Mackenzie told Neil of its imminent arrival – and Neil promptly captured it.

The king now realised he had no one to trust and would have to negotiate with Neil directly. To help the process along, Neil turned against an English pirate crew who had offered to help him clear the settlers, sending the pirates in chains to Edinburgh, where they were duly hanged on the sands at Leith.

When Mackenzie died in 1611, Neil and his followers withdrew to the isolated rock of Berisay off the west coast of Lewis, from where they carried out a vicious campaign of piracy. He was finally prised out by Mackenzie's son, Roderick, who rounded up all the female members of the families of Neil's pirates who were living on the mainland. They were tied up and put in an open boat which was rowed out to a reef in sight of Berisay. Then the boat was holed and its terrified occupants left to drown in the rising tide. The pirates set out to rescue the women, and in the resulting chaos were forced to surrender. Neil Mackenzie was hanged in Edinburgh in 1613.

Above: A map of Lewis from 1750, showing Berisay (Bearasaigh or Bearasay), the island that provided a secure fortress for Neil MacLeod and his gang in the early 1600s; and **Background**: The remains of the original Stornoway Castle, which was destroyed in 1684.

Hijackers and mutineers

The ship hijacked by the Usipi was a *liburna* (or *liburnian*) – a small galley propelled by oars and a sail, similar to this replica. The Roman navy favoured this type of boat for raiding and patrols.

The earliest recorded hijack in Scotland happened in c.AD 83.

Members of the German **Usipi** tribe were forced by the Romans to serve as soldiers in the inhospitable west coast of Scotland. Tired of being bullied, they murdered a centurion and several other officers, and hijacked three light warships, including their pilots. When one escaped, they killed the other two in case they should do the same.

With no idea of direction, or how properly to manage the ships, the hijackers sailed northwards. Every now and then they made land to take on water and food, but it was never enough. Eventually they began eating each other. When they had finished off the weakest, they drew lots for the next victim.

Driven erratically by oars, wind and tides, they sailed round the north coast of Scotland. Those who survived were finally wrecked off the north coast of Germany, where they were captured as pirates and sold into slavery.

Of the 46-strong crew on the HMS Bounty, which sailed from Portsmouth in 1787, seven were Scots.

The plan was to sail via Tahiti in the South Pacific to the West Indies, but things went badly wrong. The fate of the captain, **Lieutenant William Bligh**, and his ship HMS *Bounty* is a tale of the most famous hijack of all.

Right: William Bligh (1754–1817) was born in Devon or Cornwall, and was only seven when he was signed on to the British Royal Navy. At 22 he sailed with Captain James Cook aboard HMS *Resolution* on his third voyage to the Pacific Ocean, when Cook was killed.

On 28 April 1789, in the south-western Pacific, some of the *Bounty*'s crew mutinied, led by the master's mate **Fletcher Christian**. They put their captain, **William Bligh**, and 18 men who supported him, into the ship's seven-metre launch with some food, a compass and a quadrant, and set it adrift.

With Christian in command, the rest sailed the *Bounty* back to Tahiti, where many of them had established relationships with local women. Some chose to stay. Christian sailed eastward with the others to find refuge on the uninhabited island of Pitcairn, which had only recently been discovered. There he ran the ship aground and set it on fire.

Bligh, by an incredible feat of seamanship, managed to sail his overloaded boat 3600 miles west to Timor. A schooner took them back to Batavia (now Jakarta, capital of Indonesia), from where Bligh sailed back to England with only two of his original crew.

In 1791 the Navy, bent on retribution against the mutineers, despatched HMS *Pandora* to find them. *Pandora*'s captain arrested 14 men on Tahiti to bring back to trial.

Above: Pitcairn Island was named after 15-year-old Robert Pitcairn, a Scottish midshipman who, in 1767, first sighted the island.

Background: '*Point of no return for the mutineers!*' – an engraving by Robert Dodd, dated 1790, that shows Bligh and his crew being turned adrift from the *Bounty*.

The floating greenhouse

HMS *Bounty* was fitted out as a floating greenhouse (if you look closely, you will see plants on the boat in the engraving on the opposite page). William Bligh's orders were to dig up breadfruit plants in Tahiti and to transport them to the West Indies. Can you see a reason for this voyage?

Answer on page 40

Scots aboard HMS *Bounty*

- **William Elphinstone** (sailed with Captain Bligh), master's mate, born Edinburgh. Died in Batavia.
- **Peter Linkletter** (sailed with Bligh), quartermaster, born Shetland. Died in Batavia.
- **John Mills** (sailed with Christian), gunner's mate, born Aberdeen. Died on Pitcairn 1793, in a riot.
- **John Samuel** (sailed with Bligh), ship's clerk and Captain Bligh's batman, born Edinburgh. Returned with Bligh to England.
- **John Smith** (sailed with Bligh), able-seaman, born Stirling. Returned with Bligh to England.
- **George Stewart** (sailed with Christian), midshipman, born Orkney. Taken prisoner on Tahiti. Drowned in HMS *Pandora*.
- **James Valentine**, able-seaman, born Montrose. Died on the outward voyage.

On the return journey, *Pandora* was wrecked on a reef on 29 August. Four of the prisoners, chained up below decks, drowned. Of the rest, four were acquitted, one pardoned, two granted the king's mercy, and the other three were hanged.

While heading for the Torres Strait, *Pandora* (below) ran aground near the Great Barrier Reef and sank. Thirty-one crew members and four mutineers died, but 89 crew and ten prisoners sailed in open boats to Timor, and then on to Batavia (Jakarta). From there the prisoners were returned to England to face trial. Today, descendants of nine mutineers not reached by HMS *Pandora* still live on Pitcairn Island.

The last pirates to be hanged in Scotland died in 1822.

Their crime took place several thousand miles away, in the mid-Atlantic, on a two-masted brig *Jane* carrying a cargo of silver dollars. **Peter Heaman**, the Swedish mate, and **François Gautier,** the ship's French cook, murdered the *Jane*'s captain and James Paterson, a Scottish seaman on watch with them. They then terrorised the other four crew members, including Scots **Peter Smith** and **Robert Strachan**, into helping them in return for a share of the cargo when it was brought safely ashore.

Heaman and Gautier planned to land somewhere on an isolated beach, distribute the treasure and disperse. But the crew were panicked into scuttling the *Jane* and burying the loot on the shore near Stornoway, Isle of Lewis.

Although caught by suspicious islanders and customs officials, Heaman and Gautier might have got away with it if the *Jane*'s cabin-boy had not slipped away and told everything. At the trial, Smith, Strachan and the cabin-boy were acquitted and became witnesses for the prosecution. Heaman and Gautier were condemned to death, with their bodies given over to the anatomists in Edinburgh for dissection.

'Hardtack'

François Gautier was a ship's cook. Cooks were often sailors who had been disabled by an accident or enemy action. This naval cook was drawn by Thomas Rowlandson in 1799.

EXECUTION
of Heaman and Gautier

Accordingly, on Wednesday 9th January, 1822 ... a hurdle was drawn up opposite the main door of the Jail, into which the unfortunate men were placed, with their backs to the horse's tail ... facing the executioner, who sat opposite them, holding the end of a rope, with which they were bound, in his hands. In this manner the cart moved slowly down to Leith, accompanied by the Sheriff and surrounded with a detachment of dragoons, Sheriff and Police Officers, &c. where they were received by the Port Admiral, Clergymen, &c.

They arrived at the scaffold, which was erected on the sand opposite the Royal Naval Yard, about ten o'clock; and after spending ten or fifteen minutes in fervent prayer, they mounted the drop, where they shook hands, and again prayed earnestly for a few minutes, when the fatal sign was given, and they were instantly 'launched into eternity', amidst an immense multitude of spectators After hanging half an hour, they were cut down, and their bodies sent to Edinburgh in a cart to be dissected, in terms of their sentence.

The job of a cook aboard a ship was always of vital importance for the health of the crew. At sea for months on end, there was no means to keep food fresh. Salted meat stored in barrels, and pickled and preserved foods, formed a monotonous diet. This would be supplemented by the familiar ship's biscuits or 'hardtack', often called 'molar breakers' or 'dog biscuits' due to their texture and taste.

Kidnappers

Left: Patrick was over 90 years old when he died in c.AD 463. As patron saint of Ireland, his feast day is celebrated on 17th March every year.

How a saint, an earl and a king were all victims of pirates.

Patricius (or Patrick), later **Saint Patrick**, is believed to have spent his early life in the coastal region of Strathclyde, possibly near Dumbarton, towards the end of the fourth century AD. Of Romano-British descent, his grandfather was a priest, and his father a deacon and member of the town council. The family owned an estate, managed by slaves.

When Patrick was 15, Irish pirates raided the estate, kidnapped him and others, and sold them in Ireland as slaves. Patrick was forced to work as a shepherd. For six years he served his master, out in all weathers, often alone. One day he heard a voice, saying, '*Hear this, your ship is ready*'. Though the ship was located 200 miles away, he escaped and made his way to it.

After many adventures, Patrick finally rejoined his family before receiving a call to return to Ireland to preach the gospel.

Svein Asleiffson, who lived from c.1110–70, was a notorious Viking pirate.

Svein's father, who held land in Orkney and Caithness, was murdered in 1135. That year, during a Yuletide feast given by the overlord of these territories, **Earl Paul Haakonsson**, Svein quarrelled with the earl's cup-bearer and killed him. As punishment Paul outlawed Svein, who fled to the Hebrides before joining the household at Logierait, near Dunkeld, of Paul's estranged half-sister Margaret and her husband Madadd, the Earl of Atholl.

Earl Paul was hunting otters on the Orkney island of Rousay when Svein arrived, raging for revenge. Many of the earl's companions were killed, and Paul was taken to Logierait. He was tortured and maimed, perhaps even blinded, so that no one would bother to rescue him. It is said that Paul was then forced to give up his earldom to a Norwegian, Ragnald Kali Kolsson, in partnership with the Atholls' five-year-old son Harald Madaddson.

Svein continued his campaigns of violence, becoming rich in the process, but died in Ireland on one of his plundering trips. The people of Dublin, having submitted to him, dug pits inside the walls of the town and covered them with brushwood and straw. When Svein and his crew returned the next day to discuss the terms of surrender, they fell into the traps and were set upon by armed citizens hiding nearby. It is said that Svein Asleiffson was the last to die.

The years 1401–1405 were a terrible time for Scotland and its king, **Robert III**.

Robert's queen died. His son and heir David, Duke of Rothesay, was imprisoned in the manor of Falkland (later Falkland Palace) by Robert's brother, the Duke of Albany, who wanted the throne for himself. Then David died, possibly deliberately starved to death. As Robert's own health declined, he decided to send 11-year-old James, his second son, to safety in France, away from the influence of Albany and his supporters.

Things got worse. Sir David Fleming, the king's special councillor, accompanied James in secret to North Berwick. From there the boy was rowed out to the inhospitable Bass Rock to wait for a suitable ship. On his way back, Fleming was murdered by an associate of Albany.

It was a month before a cargo ship took James and his small party off the Rock, long enough for his departure to be reported abroad. Off the coast of Yorkshire, the ship was attacked and boarded by English pirates. King Henry IV of England returned the cargo to its owners, but kept the prince.

The news was too much for Robert III, who died soon after hearing it. James was now King of Scotland, but still a prisoner in the Tower of London. Though later allowed out and given an education at the English court, he remained captive for 18 years.

James was finally freed to return home in 1424, provided the Scots paid £40,000 to cover the cost of his board and lodging as a prisoner! He rode north, determined to be a firm ruler.

Falkland Palace

While in England, James married Lady Joan Beaufort, granddaughter of the famous John of Gaunt. On 21 May 1424, James I and his Queen were crowned properly at Perth.

Above: This picture of James I and his wife Lady Joan Beaufort was made in the 16th century. The gold signet (**below**) is Joan's Privy Seal, *c.*1425, found at Kinross.

Background: The castle on the Bass Rock, which served as a prison for some enemies of the Crown.

Bass Rock facts

- The Bass Rock is located in the Firth of Forth in the east of Scotland and is 3 hectares in size.
- Like North Berwick Law, nearby in East Lothian, the Bass Rock is the remnant of an old and extinct volcano.
- The castle on the Rock was sometimes used as a prison. During the 15th century, King James I sent political enemies there. In the 17th century, Covenanters were imprisoned in the island prison. Later, Jacobites were also incarcerated there.
- Today the island is considered a Site of Special Scientific Interest due to having the world's largest northern colony of gannets. There are also fulmars, kittiwakes, puffins, razorbills and guillemots.

Bass Rock

Privateers or pirates?

How seamen, including a duke, earl and three brothers, bent the rules in search of rich **prizes**, and how a privateer became a desert-island castaway.

Privateer was the name given to an armed ship, its owner, captain or a crew member who had been granted a government licence (**letter of marque**) to attack and rob ships of a nation with which it was at war. In peacetime, a **letter of reprisal** would be issued to allow a ship's owner or captain to seek compensation for a wrong he claimed had been done to him at sea. Privateers, with government support, were not pirates, though they often behaved as if they were!

Flanders-born **John Crab** began as a pirate, but plundered English merchant ships under the guise of a privateer.

In c.1306, during the Wars of Independence between Scotland and England, he and his nephew, Crabbekyn, attacked and robbed English merchant ships so mercilessly that King Edward II complained angrily to the Count of Flanders, who took no notice.

In about 1310, Crab settled in Aberdeen, and then in Berwick in 1318, helping to strengthen the town's defences after it had been recovered for Scotland by Robert I.

In 1332, he took ten ships to Perth to blockade Edward Balliol, who was, with the backing of Edward III, claiming the Crown of Scotland. Crab's expedition failed miserably and he was captured by the English.

Crab next turned up in 1333, on the side of the English, helping them to take Berwick by using his knowledge of its defences. After that he worked for his new master's forces in Scotland, supplying men, ships, and siege engines.

Alexander Stewart, Earl of Mar, and **Robert Davidson**, twice Provost of Aberdeen, wreaked havoc at sea for four years.

Between c.1408–12 they carried out attacks on merchant ships of the Netherlands, England, and the Hanseatic League of cities in northern Germany. The attacks were so devastating to their victims that the League imposed a ban on Scottish trade that lasted until 1436.

The Scottish armed merchantman *Yellow Carvel*, c.1475, was commanded by John Barton before it came into the ownership of James IV.

Robert Barton was also attacking English ships, which he continued to do with extra ferocity under the flag of France after Andrew's death. From 1513, however, until his death in 1540, Robert served the Scottish Crown in a variety of official and unofficial financial roles, using the vast funds he had built up from piracy to subsidise government and court expenditure.

In 1519, he even gave **Margaret Tudor**, the mother of **King James V**, a personal loan, so that she would not have to pawn her jewels to pay her household expenses.

In 1507 **James IV** issued letters of marque against Portugal to the brothers **Barton** – **Andrew**, **Robert** (or **Hob a Barton**), and **John** – whose father's ship and goods were taken by the Portuguese over thirty years before.

The brothers used the letters of marque to plunder ships of all nations, including England. Three years later, Andrew was prowling off the east coast of England. He attacked any ship that passed, claiming that its goods were Portuguese. In June 1511, two English vessels, commanded by **Lord Thomas Howard** and his brother **Sir Edward**, came across him. There was a terrible and bloody battle, in which Andrew was killed.

Whose grandmother?

Margaret Tudor (1489–1541) was the sister of King Henry VIII of England. She was married to James IV of Scotland from 1503 until his death at the Battle of Flodden in 1513, fighting against English forces. She then became Regent for their son James V of Scotland and later married Archibald Douglas, 6th Earl of Angus. Look up a family tree which includes Margaret Tudor. Can you spot who her famous grandchildren are?

Answer on page 40

The Union of the Crowns in 1603 meant that Scotland and England had one king, **James VI and I**, and, for defence, the Royal Scots Navy and the English Royal Navy.

But each country retained its own Admiralty, issuing letters of marque to privateers in wartime and letters of reprisal in times of peace.

The seas around Britain and northern Europe teemed with privateers, particularly during the Third Anglo-Dutch War in 1672–74 when Britain and France tried to take from Holland her position as leader in world trade. Dutch privateers seized *c*.650 British and French merchant ships, many of which were Scottish.

The Scots were active too. **Charles Stuart, Lord High Admiral of Scotland**, did not stick to the rules, sometimes designating the Royal Scots Navy ship *Speedwell* a privateer to suit his own personal interests.

In April 1672, Stuart was in the naval vessel *Portland* en route to Denmark to take up an ambassador's appointment. When they encountered a Dutch (enemy) merchant ship, Stuart refused to allow *Portland*'s captain to capture it. Instead, as Lord High Admiral, he hailed a passing English fishing vessel, transferred his servants on board, issued its skipper with a letter of marque, and ordered him to take the Dutch ship. Thus Stuart, and not the King of England, got the gain from the **prize** of seizing the Dutch merchantman.

Above: James VI and I (1566–1625) on a stained-glass window, 1619. **Below:** Charles Stuart, 6th Duke of Lennox and 3rd Duke of Richmond, by Sir Peter Lely, *c*.1668.

The sea, however, was also his undoing. Later that year, after a drunken dinner on board an English warship, Stuart missed his footing on the ladder down to the boat waiting to row him back to shore, and sank straight to the seabed. Crewmen managed to pull him out and give him the kiss of life, but he died later that day.

Alexander Selkirk, privateer, was born in 1676 in Lower Largo, Fife, seventh son of a shoemaker.

Though he went to sea against his father's wishes, by 1703 he was master of the galley *Cinque Ports*, which was carrying letters of marque and reprisal.

The captain, Charles Pickering, died on the coast of Brazil and was succeeded by Captain Stradling. *Cinque Ports* was then sailed round the treacherous Cape Horn, with Selkirk commended for his seamanship. But having limited success with prizes, the ship put in to the archipelago of Juan Fernández in September 1704 for a refit.

Here Selkirk became so convinced the ship was not fit to go to sea that he stated he would rather be marooned alone on the uninhabited Más a Tierra, one of the Juan Fernández islands. So a boat put him ashore with his clothes and bedding, musket, powder and bullets, tobacco, a hatchet, knife and kettle, a Bible, some odds and ends, and his mathematical instruments and tables. As the boat was leaving, Selkirk had second thoughts, but Stradling was having none of it and ordered the crew to continue rowing.

Stradling's appraisal of the state of the galley was wrong. *Cinque Ports* leaked so badly that the crew abandoned ship and took to rafts. Only 18 of them reached the mainland, where they were captured and cruelly treated by both the Spanish and the local people.

DECLARATION
by Captain Pickering, *Cinque Ports*

Appeared personally Capt Charles Pickering and produced a Warrant from His Royall Highness Prince George of Denmark etc Lord High Admiral of England Ireland etc and of all her Majesties Plantations etc for the granting of a Commission or Lettler of Marque to him the said Charles Pickering, and in pursuance of her Majesties Instructions to Privateers made the following Declaration *viz.* that his ship is called the *Cinque Ports Gally*, and is ... about one hundred & Thirty Tonnes mounted with Twenty Gunns, that he the Declarant goes Captain of her, that she carryes ninety men, One hundred small Armes, Fourty Cutlaces Thirty Six Barrells of powder, Fifty Tonnes of great shott, and about one Tonn of small shott, [and] that the said ship is victualled for four months ...

Above: A sea-chest used by Alexander Selkirk during his time on Más a Tierra, Juan Fernández.

Left: A transcript of the original letter of marque and reprisal issued to Captain Pickering, first commander of the galley *Cinque Ports*, in which Alexander Selkirk sailed as master in 1703.

Background: The cave on Más a Tierra island, Juan Fernández, where Alexander Selkirk lived for more than four years.

Below: An imaginary picture of Robinson Crusoe, a character inspired by Alexander Selkirk, as a 'man cloth'd in Goat-Skins' on a desert island.

Selkirk remained on the island for four years and four months, during which he avoided capture by a landing party from two enemy Spanish vessels who had spotted him.

He was finally taken off by the English privateer *Duke*, whose captain, **Woodes Rogers**, described him as a '*man cloth'd in Goat-Skins, who looked wilder than the first Owners of them, who had so much forgot his Language for want of Use, that we could scarce understand him, for he seem'd to speak his words by halves*'.

That was, for Selkirk, just the beginning of new adventures.

Sailing off the coast of Chile, the *Duke* took a ship as a prize. It was renamed *Increase*, with Selkirk appointed master.

After further duties at sea, Rogers' ships had a refit on the Galapagos Islands, before taking up position at the mouth of the Gulf of California to intercept a Spanish galleon en route from Manila to Acapulco. They waited for seven weeks when, with supplies of bread almost exhausted, a sail was spotted on the horizon.

They gave chase. There was a brief skirmish, but the *Duke*'s heavier, and better-manned, guns, backed up by volleys of musket-fire, prevailed. The heavily-laden galleon lowered its colours to indicate surrender. She was boarded, and renamed *Batchelor*, with Selkirk as master.

Rogers now set sail across the Pacific with all his ships. After a voyage of almost five months, they reached Batavia (Jakarta). Here there was a division of booty, with Selkirk acting as one of the presiding officials. His own share was 80 pieces of eight.

Duke, *Batchelor* and an accompanying convoy finally reached the River Thames in October 1711. Selkirk had been away over eight years, during which he had circumnavigated the world. He returned to sea in 1720, again in a privateer, but died the following year, probably of disease, off the coast of West Africa.

Pieces of eight

Pieces of eight, worth eight *reales*, were the most common Spanish silver coin. As global trade increased they became units of international currency. Their particular association with pirates probably stems from the cry 'Pieces of eight, pieces of eight' repeatedly uttered by Long John Silver's pet parrot in Robert Louis Stevenson's novel, *Treasure Island* (see page 37).

In 2005 a team of scientists and archaeologists searched Más a Tierra for traces of Selkirk's time there. They discovered the remains of a fire, animal bones, and post-holes that were later dated to about the right time. In the soil was a piece of copper 16 millimetres long, identified as one of the tips from a pair of dividers used for measuring lines on charts. Selkirk, as master of a ship, would have had an instrument like this with him on the island.

Castaway!

Selkirk's adventures on Más a Tierra inspired the author **Daniel Defoe** (1660–1731) to write his famous novel *Robinson Crusoe* (1719). Readers thought the book was a true story as the original edition appeared to be written by 'Crusoe' himself. But there are many differences between Selkirk and Crusoe. Selkirk's four-year stay is a lot shorter than Crusoe's 28 years; and Crusoe was shipwrecked, not left behind at his own request.

William Davidson was the Scottish keeper of an unusual diary.

While serving on board Royal Navy ship *Niger*, Davidson was convicted for drunkenness and insolence, and then for striking an officer. A search of his sea-chest revealed a handwritten diary, *The Bloody Journal Kept by William Davidson on Board a Russian Pirate in the Year 1789*. If genuine, it is a record of a year in a Russian privateer, *Saint Dinnan*, which cruised along the coast of Asia Minor.

After robbing numerous Turkish ships and murdering their crews, the so-called privateers plundered some of the small Greek islands in the vicinity. They also attacked another pirate ship, whose crew of more than 300 were captured and massacred.

Davidson deserted from the *Niger* in 1793, but was later pressganged into serving again, as a gunner, on HMS *Royal George*. He was accidentally drowned in 1797.

The tale of Mary Jones, 'pirate slayer'.

John Fullarton, a ship's captain from Orkney, was said to be one of the most infamous of the 18th-century privateers. At first he operated legitimately in time of war, but Fullarton soon became greedy and turned to piracy in peacetime. After many bloody but successful actions, he came across a heavily-loaded Scottish merchant ship, *Isabella*, in the Firth of Forth.

When **Captain Jones**, in charge of the *Isabella*, refused to surrender, a fierce battle ensued. Only when the ship's mast had been shot away was Fullarton able to board her. He was so angry with Jones that he shot him. **Mary Jones**, the captain's wife, also onboard, grabbed a pistol, put it against Fullarton's forehead and pressed the trigger, killing him stone dead.

Below: 'Manning the Navy' by pressganging was the practice of 'pressing men' who refused to volunteer for the Navy, by threat or force.

Patriot or pirate?

The tale of the Scottish sailor who joined the American Navy and raided the British coast.

John Paul was born in 1747 in Kirkcudbrightshire, southwest Scotland, and went to sea, aged 13, as an apprentice on board a ship. Though a decent sailor, his temper sometimes got the better of him. After he killed two of his fellow crew members, in 1770 and 1773, he fled to America, adding **Jones** to his name.

When the American Revolutionary War broke out in 1775, Jones joined the Continental Navy to fight against the British. Quickly rising through the ranks, by 1778 he and his crew were capturing and destroying small ships off the coast of Britain and Ireland.

He even raided Kirkcudbright Bay, just up the coast from his home town! It was his plan to capture the **Earl of Selkirk** nearby and exchange him for captured American sailors. When Jones found the earl was not at home, he stole his silver instead.

But by 1779 Jones' luck ran out. While trying to hold Leith Harbour to ransom, a gale blew his ship right out of the Firth of Forth.

John Paul Jones is celebrated in America as the founder of the newly-created United States Navy and he received a gold medal for his service during the war. But in the British press he was labelled a pirate because of his attacks on British ships.

Above: John Paul Jones (1747–92) was born in Kirkcudbright, but was most famous for his founding role in the United States Navy.

Right: A pocket watch said to have been given to John Paul by the Craik family, who owned the estate in Kirkcudbright where he grew up.

Scottish pirates of the Golden Age

Below: A flintlock belt pistol from Aberdeenshire, *c.*1700.

Famous names and dramatic but lawless acts in the years *c.*1680–1730, known as the 'Golden Age of Pirates'.

Captain 'Red Legs' Greaves was born in Barbados. His father was a Scot who had been transported as a slave, probably in the aftermath of the uprising of the Covenanters against the government in 1666. Greaves too was brought up a slave, but he escaped as a teenager by swimming across Carlisle Bay in Antigua and stowing away on a ship.

Unfortunately for Greaves it was a pirate ship. The commander, **Captain Hawkins**, was exceptionally cruel, even by pirate standards. Forced to sign the **Articles of Regulation**, the pirate's code of conduct, or face death by pistol, hatchet or cutlass, Greaves became a pirate.

It was probably his suffering as a slave that led Greaves to refuse to kill unnecessarily or to torture prisoners, but his experience of hard work also made him an excellent pirate who demonstrated powers of leadership.

Inevitably, Greaves and Hawkins fell out. Hawkins died during a fight, and Greaves was elected captain in his place. He is thought to have introduced new Articles, with punishment for the abuse of prisoners or women.

Greaves captured an entire island, Margarita, off the Venezuelan coast, using clever tactics. He overpowered the Spanish ships in the bay and turned their guns against the island's forts. He then stormed the defences, and took away a massive haul of pearls and gold,

Captain 'Red Legs' Greaves

There are a number of theories as to how Greaves got his nickname. One is that in action he used to wear a Highland plaid, which left his legs bare. If he did, this may have been an anti-government statement. Poor white people of Barbados were also called 'Redlegs', probably a reference to sunburn caused by working in the fields.

without subjecting the town or inhabitants to anything more than inconvenience.

With his share of the spoils, Greaves retired to become a planter on the Caribbean island of Nevis, a British settlement since 1628. There was still, however, a reward for his capture. A former shipmate or victim gave him away and he was tried and sentenced to be hanged.

While awaiting execution in Cotton Ground, the island's principal place of settlement, an earthquake devastated the area. Greaves took the opportunity to escape and was rescued by a whaling ship.

It is said that Greaves eventually became a pirate hunter. He was pardoned for his crimes and died in respectable old age.

If Greaves managed to live until his retirement, William Kidd was not so lucky.

Kidd was probably born in Greenock in the west of Scotland, and is said to have been the son of a Church of Scotland minister. He was already a pirate when appointed captain of a British privateer to harry French ships in the West Indies. His men, who preferred straightforward piracy, hijacked the ship in New York and stole what booty Kidd had managed to acquire for himself.

In New York he married, remained a privateer, and made friends with influential politicians and merchants, including fellow Scot **Robert Livingston**. With the help of **Richard Coote**, **Earl of Bellomont**, who had been appointed Governor of New York, the trio devised a cunning scheme.

Kidd's skills of seamanship would be used to make vast profits for a consortium of British ministers of the Crown, with King William III himself a secret partner. Kidd, armed with the necessary documents they provided, would cruise the Indian Ocean, capturing troublesome pirates and their booty, and attacking French merchant ships to relieve them of their cargoes. All the prizes would go to the 'partnership'.

Captain William Kidd

The infamous pirate on the deck of *Adventure Galley*, by American artist and writer Howard Pyle (1853–1911).

Kidd was given a powerful ship, *Adventure Galley*, and a skilled crew was enlisted, mainly pirates, in London and New York. They arrived in Madagascar from New York in January 1697 and sailed to the Red Sea, hoping to plunder ships loaded with rich cargoes and carrying pilgrims returning from the holy site of Mecca. But the ships were strongly protected and Kidd was forced to withdraw.

The *Adventure Galley's* crew were employed on a 'no prize, no pay' basis. After a couple of failed attacks off the west coast of India, and with the ship leaking badly, they became mutinous. Kidd argued with his gunner, **William Moore**, and struck him on the head with a bucket reinforced with iron hoops. Moore died and the crew backed down. For a while at least, it looked as though Kidd's fortunes were reviving.

Quedah Merchant was owned by Armenians from the shore of the Black Sea. She had an English captain, **John Wright**, and was carrying a vast cargo, including cash, silk, calico, sugar, iron and opium, much of which was the property of a minister of the Mogul of India.

Kidd intercepted *Quedah Merchant* in the Arabian Sea and closed in, falsely flying a French flag at his masthead. Wright sent over a boat with a French pass, indicating that he was exempt from the attentions of French privateers. Kidd took the pass and produced his own letters of marque, authorising him to attack French ships. His aggressive manner and potential fire-power won the day. Wright's ship was seized and the cargo sold at the nearest suitable port.

Kidd then captured five more ships, only one of which was carrying a French pass. But now his luck began to run out.

Adventure Galley sank off the coast of Madagascar, though he still had *Quedah Merchant*. Then influential authorities in India complained to the British government about pirate activities off their shores, and in particular about William Kidd. An order was issued for his arrest.

Back in New York, Kidd appealed to his consortium partners Livingston and Bellomont, but they offered no help. Instead, Bellomont had Kidd returned to England as a prisoner, with as much of his booty as could be found.

Captain William Kidd was executed on 23 May 1701, twice. First time, the rope broke and had to be replaced. The prison chaplain, **Revd Paul Lorrain**, attempted to extract a last confession, but to no avail. Kidd was strung up a second and final time and his body left hanging in chains on Execution Dock beside the River Thames as a warning to others.

After being held in London's Newgate jail for almost a year, Kidd was examined in the House of Commons before the assembled members of Parliament. There was no one there to defend him because his partners in the scheme belonged to the political party that was now out of office. Kidd was taken back to jail to await his fate.

The trial of Captain William Kidd took place on 8 and 9 May 1701. His defence against the charge of piracy was that his actions had been against French ships, and as proof he asked for the two French passes he had taken to be returned to him. But the evidence had rather strangely disappeared and was not unearthed until the 20th century.

Kidd was found guilty of piracy and of the murder of William Moore and was sentenced to be hanged. Author Daniel Defoe, then an undercover journalist, wrote that on hearing the sentence, Kidd protested: '*My Lord, it is a very hard sentence. For my part I am the innocentest Person of them all, only I have been sworn against by perjured Persons.*'

THE BALLAD of Captain Kidd

To the *Execution Dock*,
I must go, I must go
To the *Execution Dock*, I must go,
To the *Execution Dock*,
While many *thousands* flock,
But I must bear the *shock*,
And I must die.

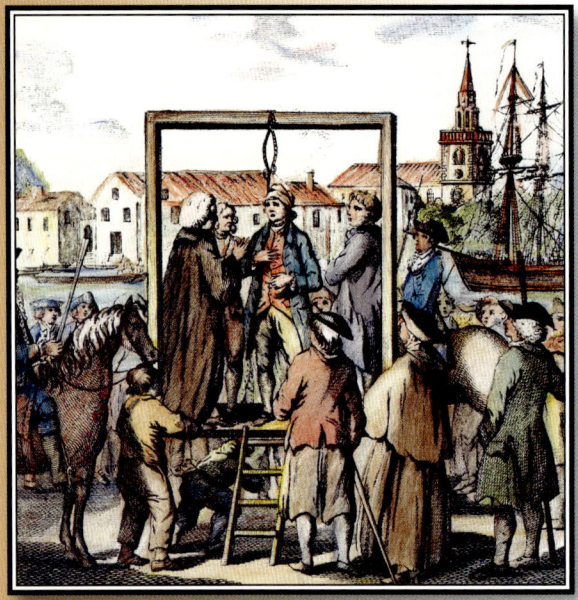

Left: This 18th-century engraving shows a pirate being hanged at Execution Dock, beside the River Thames. The prison chaplain stands in front of the prisoner to hear any words of confession.

the crew and throwing them all overboard. This time he could not escape the noose.

On the scaffold Dolzell was rude to the chaplain, Revd Paul Lorrain, though he did eventually repent his sins and apologise for his behaviour. Lorrain was unimpressed and considered Dolzell a man of a '*morose, stubborn and ill disposition by nature*'.

In 1715 **Captain Alexander Dolzell (Dalziel)**, a 42-year-old Scot, encountered the same fate as William Kidd.

Dolzell's tale is full of dastardly deeds. It was said that he once overpowered a Spanish war galleon whose captain had retired to his cabin for a game of cards, not imagining that the Scot would attack. Dolzell, however, had drilled a hole in the side of his own ship, forcing his crew to board the galleon.

Later Dolzell served as a French privateer, causing great damage to British shipping. Captured and taken back to England, he was convicted of high treason and sentenced to be hanged, drawn and quartered.

Somehow he obtained a royal pardon, but went back to his old ways and attacked a French ship in the English Channel, tying up

David Sympson

Below is an engraving (1841) of Cape Coast Castle on the Atlantic coast of what is now Ghana. In about 1722, inside the castle, a sensational trial took place of 169 pirates, the greatest number ever tried together. Fifty-three were marched to the scaffold outside the castle gates and hanged. Of these, four were Scots, including a prize catch – **David Sympson**, from North Berwick, known as 'Lord' Sympson. He claimed the title as one of the original leaders of the pirates who congregated at New Providence, Bahamas, in about 1715.

John Gow, alias **Smith**, born in the Orkney Islands, was one of the most incompetent of the pirate captains of the 'Golden Age'.

Brought up in Stromness, Orkney, he seems to have run away to sea, and early on to have aspired to become a pirate captain. For this, however, he needed a ship.

Gow's first attempt to hijack the ship, on which he was serving as boatswain, failed because he could not enlist enough help from the crew. His second, in 1724, was more successful, but not without bloodshed. At that time he was second mate in the 22-gun merchant vessel *Caroline*, commanded by Captain Ferneau and sailing from the Canary Islands to Genoa, Italy.

One night, he and six others, including another Scot, **William Melvin**, slit the throats of the captain, surgeon, chief mate, and ship's clerk. None died instantly, so they were shot as they crawled about the deck, and their bodies tossed overboard. The rest of the crew were threatened with similar treatment if they did not toe the line.

With the ship renamed *Revenge,* and Gow appointed captain, the intrepid band of amateur pirates cruised around the coasts, looking for booty. They had mixed luck. Two of the ships they took were carrying just fish, but others yielded some meagre plunder and a few recruits to the crew.

Centre: A sword from the 18th century.

Below: Typical woodcut book illustration of the time said to represent Gow, taken from Daniel Defoe's *A General History of the Robberies and Murders of the most notorious pyrates* (1724).

The fish came in useful, though, when Gow put in to the Portuguese island of Porto Santo to take on water and supplies. Flying an English flag, Gow conned the Governor of the island into thinking he was a merchantman by sending him a gift of three barrels of salmon and six of herring.

The Governor was charmed, until on a courtesy visit to the *Revenge* he and his party were taken prisoner at gun-point, and informed that they would only be released when the supplies arrived.

After a few more largely unprofitable raids, the crew became disgruntled with Gow. With the ship now named *George Galley*, he sailed for Orkney where he hoped to replenish supplies, re-fit the ship, and scrape its hull of weeds and barnacles – all without being detected by the authorities.

Several of his crew deserted and informed the authorities of Gow's presence. With the hull only half scraped, Gow quickly set sail, not for freedom but for the island of nearby Graemsay, between the mainland and Hoy. Here he hoped to plunder the estate of Robert Honeyman, High Sheriff of Orkney.

Honeyman was away, investigating reports of pirates in the area. His wife and daughter fled with most of their gold, leaving the pirates barely seven pounds in cash and some silver spoons. As they left, Gow's men abducted two servant girls, and the piper to the estate for good measure.

Still Gow would not give up. He sailed north, round the mainland of Orkney, to the island of Eday, to plunder the home of Mr Fea, a rich landowner whom he had known when they were schoolboys together. But the ship got into difficulties and ran aground. Gow had to ask for Fea's assistance, but instead, after inviting the boatswain and four companions for a drink, Fea had them seized.

When the ship ran aground again, Gow observed prophetically, '*We are all dead men!*' Sure enough, Gow and his crew were captured and taken to London.

At the trial, Gow refused to state he was guilty or not guilty, even after agonising pressure had been put upon his thumbs by an executioner. The judge then ordered him to be 'pressed', although when he realised what that meant a not-guilty plea was quickly forthcoming.

John Gow was hanged on 11 June 1725. As in the case of Kidd, the rope broke after he had hung for four minutes. Seemingly unconcerned, Gow climbed up the ladder and was hanged again.

Right: Thumbikins, or thumbscrews, 1700.

Below: Pressing a pirate. Punishment from medieval times involving weights being piled upon the body until the victim either confesses or dies.

Pirate hunters

Tackling pirate ships at sea.

The years 1489–90 were especially busy for pirate hunters. Their quarry came not just from the mainland of Europe for, as England and Scotland were officially at peace, English attacks on Scottish ships and land counted as piracy too.

Sir Andrew Wood (c.1455–1539), a sea captain from Leith, served King James IV well in the pursuit of pirates. In 1489 five English ships brazenly entered the Firth of Forth, inflicting terrible damage on shore and to merchant ships sailing to and from Leith and other ports nearby. Wood's ships, *Yellow Carvel* and *Flower* (right), caught up with the English pirates off Dunbar, engaged in battle, and escorted the captured ships in triumph back to Leith.

The English king, Henry VII, was furious and sent three specially-equipped privateers, under Stephen Bull, to bring Wood in, dead or alive. Bull lay in wait for Wood to return from a trip to Flanders, and swept down on his two ships off St Abb's Head, Eyemouth. After an epic two-day battle, ending at the mouth of the River Tay far up the east coast, Wood claimed the victory.

Sir Andrew Wood's victory

Robert Lindsay of Pitscottie (born c.1532) wrote a graphic account of Wood's epic sea-battle in *Historie and Cronikles of Scotland*.

The night sundred [parted] them, that they were fain [glad] to depart from other. While, on the morn, that the day began to break fair, and their trumpets to blow on every side, and made them quickly to battle; who clapt [fastened] together, and fought so cruelly, that neither the shippers nor mariners took heed of their ships; but fighting still, while an ebb tide and south-wind bure [bore] them to Inchcap[e Rock]*, foreanents [opposite] the mouth of the Tay. The Scottish-men, seeing this, took courage and hardiment, that they doubled their strokes upon the English-men; and had them up to the town of Dundee.

*Inchcape Rock is now the site of the famous Bell Rock lighthouse.

Battles at sea

The tiny fishing port of Anstruther in Fife witnessed extraordinary scenes in 1587. Local minister, **James Melville**, wrote an account of them.

Since ancient times, sea-battles were fought like land battles. Guns were set up on deck to shoot away the enemy's sails and rigging. Boarding parties stood by with grappling irons and hooks. Crossbowmen climbed up to cages at the tops of masts, shooting downwards on the opposition. Hand-to-hand combatants, officers in full armour, the rest in reinforced jackets and steel caps, all fought on a platform created by the locked hulls.

While sailing home from England, a Scottish ship was attacked and plundered offshore by English pirates, and a seaman from Anstruther killed. When a second ship, at anchor at neighbouring Pittenweem, was also struck, furious townsmen decided to fight back. They rigged out a fast ship of their own, raised the king's standard, and '*encouraging each other, almost the whole honest and best men in the town* [went] *in her to sea*'.

Alongside a ship from St Andrews they met on the way, the Anstruther crew sailed down the east coast of England in pursuit of the English pirates. On the way, they dismasted an English merchant ship with a single gun-shot, when it refused to '*do homage to the king of Scotland*'.

Then, off the Suffolk coast, they spotted the very pirate ship that had caused the original trouble, just as it was plundering *another* Anstruther ship. A battle began, with gunfire so loud that people on shore thought their enemies from Spain had landed!

The local Suffolk magistrates, spotting the king's standard, took the Scots' side against the pirates. James Melville wrote, they were allowed to '*take with them their prisoners and pirate's ship; whereof two were hanged on our pier-end, the rest at St Andrews; with nae hurt to any of our folks,* [who ever since] *have been free from English pirates*'.

In August 1720, Ayrshire-born **Captain James Macrae** (1677–1744) was in charge of the *Cassandra*, an armed merchant vessel on hire to the East India Company ferrying goods between Britain and the East.

Above: Born Edward Seegar in Ireland, c.1685, England sailed the coasts of Africa and the Indian Ocean as captain of a pirate ship from 1717–20.

Sailing from the Mozambique Channel, off Madagascar, with two armed escorts – the Company's *Greenwich* and a Dutch ship – Macrae spotted two other vessels sailing towards him, under the command of the notorious Irish pirate, **Edward England**.

The larger ship, *Victory*, was flying England's standard, the skull and crossbones on a black background, but also a red flag. This signalled that resistance would mean death to those taken prisoner.

Cassandra carried 30 guns and, with its two escorts should have had the greater firepower. Instead, the escorts stood out to sea and watched, leaving *Cassandra* to take on the pirates alone. During a bloody three-hour battle, so many on board Macrae's ship were killed or wounded that the captain gave orders for the able-bodied to abandon ship. Most reached the shore safely, in boats or by swimming.

Macrae later wrote: '*When the Pyrates came aboard, they cut three of our wounded Men to Pieces; I, with a few of my People, made what Haste I could to the King's Town, twenty five miles from us, where I arrived next day … having been sorely wounded in the Head by a Musket Ball.*'

Bravely, Macrae returned ten days later to face the pirates who had brutally killed his men. He asked for his ship, so that the survivors could return home. England kept *Cassandra*, but allowed Macrae one of the pirate's vessels, which was in a terrible state. Macrae's depleted crew repaired it as best they could and set sail, finally reaching Bombay (Mumbai), India, 48 days later.

Pirate doctors

Scottish doctors aboard pirate ships included **Lionel Wafer**, **Archibald Murray**, **Robert Hunter** and **John Hincher**.

Above: An illustration from Wafer's book *A New Voyages and Description of the Isthmus of America* (1699), based on his time in Panama.

Lionel Wafer, a Gaelic speaker, started out as surgeon's assistant on a merchant vessel. He then worked as a surgeon in Jamaica, before becoming a pirate by choice.

In 1681, after a raid on Panama, Wafer was badly injured when a barrel of gunpowder blew up. Cared for by the local Cuna Indians, he studied their medical traditions and noted his observations in a book later written about the geography, natural history and culture of the region.

Once fit, Wafer took part in pirate skirmishes off the coasts of North and South America and in the South Seas. In 1688, he was arrested but released, even though 37 silver plates, silver lace and three bags of Spanish cash were found among his possessions.

Back in Britain, Wafer, now regarded as an expert on the South American region, was invited to advise the directors of what turned out to be a disastrous Scottish expedition to the Darien isthmus in Panama, in which over 2000 settlers died. He had been expected to travel with them, but in the end he did not go. Wafer died at fifty in London in 1705.

The Darien Scheme

In the 17th century, Scotland expanded both economically and culturally. Trading abroad increased and with it the ambition to found a Scottish colony.

The Darien Scheme, funded by Scots, made a disastrous choice of location for its expeditions of 1698 and 1699, landing in the swampy regions of Central America. The resultant financial collapse of the Scheme, and the dire economic effect on the country, was a critical factor in the negotiations that led to the Union of the Parliaments of Scotland and England in 1707.

Dr Archibald Murray, from an ancient family in the Scottish Borders, was first captured by pirates in 1718.

Murray was surgeon aboard the *Buck*, a ship fitted out as a pirate-hunting privateer by Woodes Rogers, at that time Governor of the Bahamas (see page 18).

Some of the *Buck's* crew of former pirates mutinied, hijacking the ship and those of its crew who could be persuaded to join them. Dr Murray disappeared at this point, only to mysteriously reappear in 1720 as a member of the pirate crew of the *Eagle*, claiming that he had been a prisoner all this time.

The *Eagle*, now foundering off the coast of Argyll, had originally been captured by pirates while sailing from the West Indies to Virginia in America. As members of the crew had escaped into the countryside, the Scottish authorities went to recover booty left behind on the ship. They were astonished to find 3000 Portuguese gold coins, 2000 English gold guineas, 200 ounces of powdered gold and a mass of jewellery.

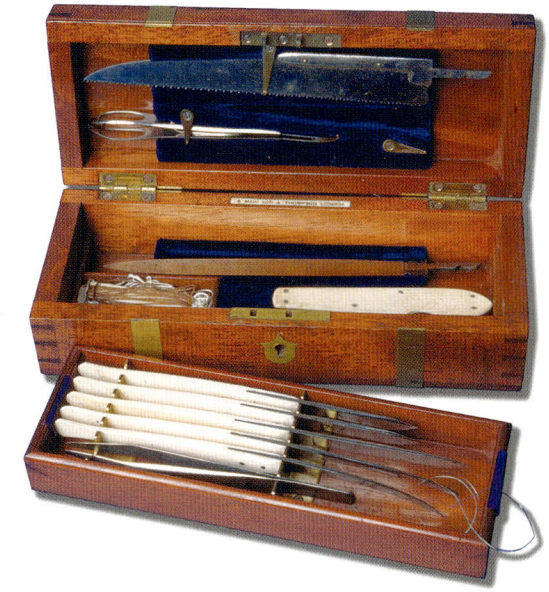

On 3 November 1720, 17 of the pirate crew stood trial in Edinburgh, but Dr Murray was not included. He had been granted a full pardon for agreeing to testify against them.

The prosecution produced sensational evidence that these men were hardened pirates who had arrived in Scotland after committing a series of atrocities off the coast of West Africa. The defence tried to argue that even so, they were all forced men captured at sea and compelled to be pirates. Despite this, ten of the prisoners were found guilty and hanged in batches on the shore at Leith.

Above: Surgical instruments used at sea, *c.*18th century.

Below: Leith Harbour, *c.*1693. Leith Sands, near Edinburgh, was the site of many pirate hangings.

In January 1722, the merchant ship *Greyhound* from Boston was captured in the Bay of Honduras by the pirate **Captain George Lowther** in his ship *Happy Delivery*.

Greyhound refused to submit, and when the pirates finally came aboard they roughed up the crew, including the Scots **John Crawford**, the surgeon, and **Charles Harris**, second mate, who were forced to join them.

Later that year, **Dr Robert Hunter** from Kilmarnock was taken by Lowther off the *Jeremiah & Anne* near Bermuda and made to serve in *Happy Delivery*. He was freed in October 1723 while Lowther was trapped on land, having his ship cleaned on an island off the coast of northern Venezuela. Lowther got away, but was later found dead with a pistol beside him and a bullet in his head. Twelve of his crew were caught, including two Scots. They were tried on the island of St Kitts, found guilty and hanged.

Lowther's second-in-command was **Edward 'Ned' Low**, who in May 1722 was promoted to captain of another ship, *Fancy*. Surgeon on board was **John Hincher**, graduate of Edinburgh University, whom Low had captured. Later Hincher was later transferred to *Ranger*, now captained by Charles Harris.

By 1723 *Fancy* and *Ranger* were damaging shipping off the coast of north America, when on 10 June they were intercepted and attacked by another *Greyhound*, this time a British man-of-war. Although together the two pirate ships had more guns than *Greyhound*, Low fled and Harris was captured.

Charles Harris and his crew were put on trial at Newport, Rhode Island. Dr Hincher was released, but 25 men, including Harris, were hanged.

Left: George Lowther stands by while his ship is careened (turned on its side for cleaning, caulking or sealing any gaps, and other repairs) during a stop at Port Mayo in the Gulf of Matique.

Above: Edward 'Ned' Low in the midst of a hurricane.

Ballads and books

Pirates appear in all kinds of literature – from broadsides, poems and novels, to today's media and blockbuster films.

In the 18th century, **broadsides** (or **broadsheets**) were single sheets of paper, printed on one side only. They were supplied and read unfolded, or were posted up in public places. At the beginning of the 18th century they took the place of today's popular press, and were used particularly for ballads and scaffold speeches.

The broadsheet extract (right) tells of the heroic feats of **Captain Thomas Gordon** (1658–1741), who commanded the Scottish naval vessel *Royal Mary*, specially equipped to protect Scotland's east coast from French privateers. In 1704, when the events celebrated here took place, Gordon captured the *Marmedon* of Dunkirk, and brought his prize in to Leith.

Captain Gordon's 'Welcome Home'

Now Brave Captain Gordon's come,
And brought more Prizes with him home
... Because where ever he appears,
He clears Our Coasts of Privateers,
Makes Merchant Ships Trade without fears
Through out the Northern Ocean.
... Of Sterling pounds, so that I hope.
We'r almost alike with the English Fop,
Who did our Africk Annandale stop,
Into the Southern Ocean;–
... Too, too long we have silent been,
Too many abuses have we seen,
Since Our King did Succeed their Queen;
And both Lands made an Union.
Yet England still to Scotland broke.
In every thing they undertook,
Designing to keep's under Yoak
And void of their Communion.
... Now since that Heaven hath set us free
Strive to maintain your Libertie.
And suffer no more slaverie
But let's unite together,
With Heart and Hand firmly to Stand,
In defence of this Ancient Land
That they may you no more command,
Who would deceive their Brother.
... So shall we live in joy and peace,
And happy make Our future race
That it may be told in each place,
Scotland Renews Her Honour,
By keeping close to our Ancient Right,
And Liberty, with all her might.
While Sun and Moon do give their Light
Let Scots Men shew their Valour.

Left: Gordon was a Jacobite, a supporter of King James VII & II and his heirs. When the German-born George I, Queen Anne's second cousin, came to the throne in 1714, Gordon refused to take the oath of allegiance to the Crown and resigned his commission. Joining the Russian Navy in 1717, he was promoted to admiral in 1727 and died in Russia in 1741.

Later that year, Captain Gordon captured several more privateers, and temporarily solved that particular problem.

The *Annandale* mentioned in the ballad on page 35 was a Scottish ship seized in 1704, off the south coast of England by representatives of the East India Company. This prevented the ship from carrying out its legitimate business of sailing via the Cape of Good Hope (South Africa) into the Indian Ocean.

It was a time of heated debate about the likelihood of the Scottish and English parliaments being united (this took place in 1707). In particular, the Scots were furious at what they saw as their betrayal by King William over the Darien Scheme in 1698 (see page 32). Many of them (known as Jacobites) believed fervently that the legitimate ruler of England and Scotland was not William, nor his sister-in-law Queen Anne, who succeeded him in 1702, but James Edward Stuart, son of James VII (and II of England), and his second wife.

This, and other causes for dissent, are reflected in the broadside ballad in its threats of invasion, slavery, tyranny, and liberty.

And so, in retaliation for the capture of the *Annandale*, the Scots seized an English ship, the *Worcester*.

The *Worcester* had put in to Fraserburgh harbour, north-east Scotland, for repairs and supplies. Under the command of its captain, **Thomas Green**, it was trading on behalf of the East India Company.

Green and 14 members of his crew were subsequently arrested and charged with acts of piracy against unknown vessels in the Indian Ocean, thousands of miles away. The charges were false but, with one exception, all were found guilty and condemned to death.

The first to be hanged on the shore at Leith were Green, John Madder (First Mate), and John Simpson (Gunner). Green was an Englishman; **John Madder** and **John Simpson** were Scots.

A ballad, written as though by Thomas Green, finishes with this dire warning:

> Let this to all hellish Villains hereafter prove.
> A warning from falling into such crimes, least Jove
> Pursue them with vengeance as he hath done Green
> And his Bloody Crue [Crew], whose practice has been,
> Of a long time to live by Piracie, and Murther [Murder], which we sufficiently see;
> To be most clear and evidently proven
> Let Green and his Crue to the Gallows be drive[n.]

Three famous Scottish authors wrote stories featuring pirates.

Sir Walter Scott (1772–1832), lawyer, poet and novelist, wrote *The Pirate* in 1821. The pirate character is **Clement Cleveland**.

Shipwrecked **Captain Cleveland** is saved from drowning off Shetland. There he falls in love with Minna Troil and longs to give up piracy. But when his pirate ship *Revenge* arrives, his crew have other ideas ….

Sir J. M. (James Matthew) Barrie (1860–1937) was a playwright and novelist who wrote the play *Peter Pan* (1904) and the novel *Peter and Wendy* in 1911. His pirate character is known as **Captain Hook**.

Peter Pan, 'The Boy Who Wouldn't Grow Up', lives in Neverland with a tribe of Lost Boys. His enemy is **Captain Hook**, whose hand he cut off and fed to a crocodile. The crocodile wants the rest of Hook, but has swallowed a clock which warns Hook of danger with its loud 'tick-tock' …

Robert Louis Stevenson (1850–94), poet, novelist and essayist, wrote *Treasure Island* in 1883. His famous pirate character is **Long John Silver**.

In a tale of buccaneers, a map and buried gold, **Long John Silver**, a one-legged pirate masquerading as a sea cook, hijacks the *Hispaniola* and sails with his crew to Treasure Island. For cabin-boy Jim Hawkins, adventures lie ahead ….

Pirate punishment

Pirates inflicted savage punishments on one another, as well as on their captives.

Marooning
Disobedient pirates or captives were put ashore, often on lonely islands, and left to fend for themselves.

The cat-o-nine-tails
The end of a length of rope was separated into nine strands, either knotted or tipped with fish hooks. This was used to whip someone on the bare back. After the lashing, wounds might be rubbed with salt to increase the pain.

Keel hauling
The victim was weighted, tied with rope and hauled under the keel from one side of the ship to the other. Few survived injuries or slow drowning.

Hanging
This was the punishment for convicted pirates. Often the gallows were erected on the shore, so that the body was submerged at high tide. The main locations were at **Leith Sands**, and at **Execution Dock** in London. Corpses might be tarred and displayed to frighten others.

Poetic Punishment

There are references to pirate punishment in the 15th-century poem 'The Flyting [Quarrel] of Dunbar and Kennedy', a series of insults between **William Dunbar** (1459–1520), Scottish poet and courtier, and his friend **Walter Kennedy** (1455–1518).

In 'The Flyting' we read of 'Danes stretched on wheels', referring to the execution of Lutkyn Mere, a Danish pirate, and his crew in 1489. The next year, the ship *Katherine*, with a very seasick Dunbar on board, was captured by French pirates but released on payment of ransom.

Modern piracy

The most sensational naval mutiny of more recent times happened in Scottish waters.

In 1931, at a time of economic recession, the Atlantic Fleet was stationed at Invergordon on the Cromarty Firth. As part of its campaign to combat a worldwide economic recession, the coalition government of the day proposed a pay cut of 25 per cent for Naval seamen – and tempers flared.

With the fleet due to sail on exercises, battleships were brought to a standstill because some of their crews refused to obey orders. The exercises were cancelled, the government announced a temporary amnesty for any mutineers, and the ships returned to their home bases at Chatham and Portsmouth in England.

There were several outcomes. Pay-cuts were restricted to 10 per cent, some leaders of the mutiny were sent to jail, and 200 seamen were dismissed from the Navy. In an attempt to blot out from memory the so-called **Invergordon Mutiny**, the Atlantic Fleet was renamed the Home Fleet (below).

20th-century hijacking

The most recent Scottish hijack was in 1970. After threatening their captain, five of the crew of the Aberdeen fishing vessel *Mary Craig* (**left**), put him and the four other seamen ashore at Peterhead. They then took control of the boat until they were forced to give themselves up to the authorities. All five were convicted of piracy, and sent to jail.

ANSWERS

Page 9: **HMS *Bounty*** – William Bligh's orders were to bring back breadfruit plants from Tahiti to create a hardy crop of food for the slaves on the plantations in the West Indies. The War of Independence had halted the supplies of food from North America.

Page 15: **Margaret Tudor (1489–1541)** – was the daughter of Henry VII of England, wife of James IV of Scotland, mother of James V, and grandmother to Mary, Queen of Scots and her second husband, Henry, Lord Darnley.

PLACES OF INTEREST

- Aberdeen, Maritime Museum – www.aagm.co.uk/Visit/AberdeenMaritimeMuseum
- Anstruther, Scottish Fisheries Museum – www.scotfishmuseum.org
- Dumbarton, Denny Ship Model experiment tank (Scottish Maritime Museum) – www.scottishmaritimemuseum.org/dumbarton-museum
- Edinburgh, National Museums Scotland – www.nms.ac.uk
- Edinburgh, The People's Story Museum, Royal Mile – www.edinburghmuseums.org.uk/peoples-story-museum
- Glasgow, The Tall Ship (Riverside Museum) – www.thetallship.com
- Irvine, Linthouse Museum (Scottish Maritime Museum) – www.scottishmaritimemuseum.org/irvine-museum
- London, Royal Museums Greenwich – www.rmg.co.uk

Above, left: Lantern, used in the Tay Lighthouse, Firth of Tay; and (**above, right**) octant, used for navigation at sea by Alexander McKay, master of the Glasgow ship *Sydney* when it sailed from Leith to Demerara, South America, in 1864.

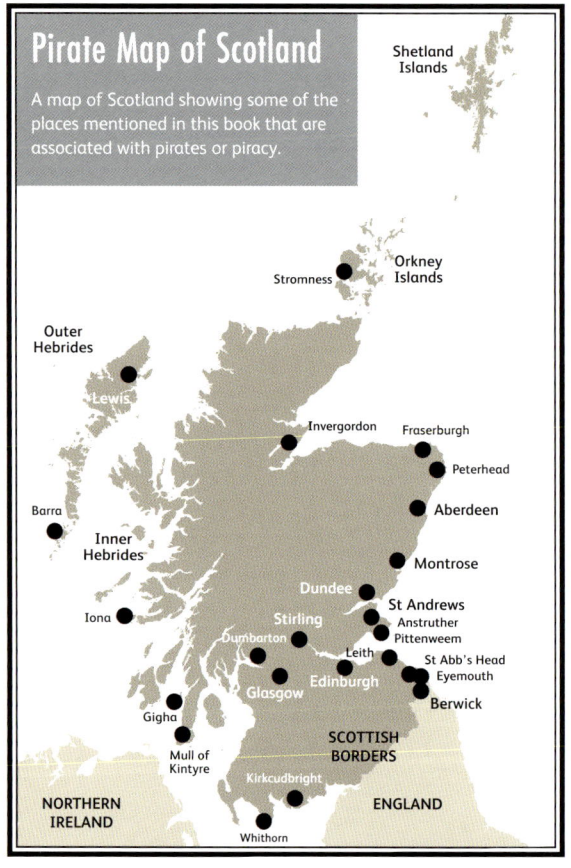

Pirate Map of Scotland

A map of Scotland showing some of the places mentioned in this book that are associated with pirates or piracy.

Pirate Tales in Scotland
Facts and activities

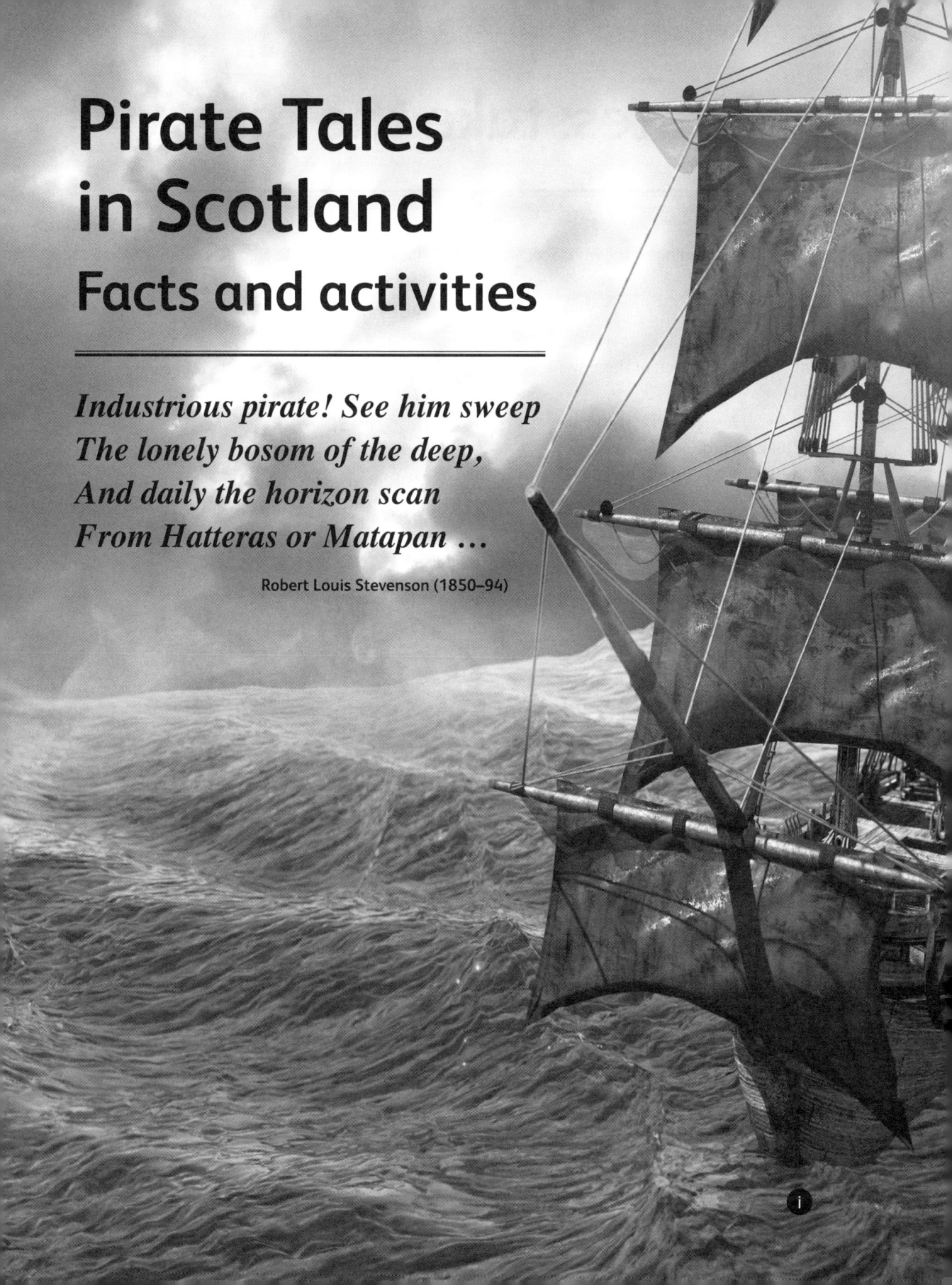

*Industrious pirate! See him sweep
The lonely bosom of the deep,
And daily the horizon scan
From Hatteras or Matapan …*

Robert Louis Stevenson (1850–94)

Pirates: take the test

1. The original meaning of the word *Scot* was 'pirate'.
   TRUE / FALSE

2. Fact or fiction? Which of these were real pirates?
   - (a) Henry Avery
   - (b) Blackbeard
   - (c) Ann Bonny
   - (d) Mary Read
   - (e) Captain Hook
   - (f) The Pirates of Penzance
   - (g) Sir Ralph the Rover
   - (h) Long John Silver

3. English-speaking pirates terrorised the Caribbean between 1715 and 1725. The percentage of these pirates who were Scottish was:
   - (a) 50 %
   - (b) 20 %
   - (c) 10 %
   - (d) 3 %

4. Some pirates had a wooden leg.
   TRUE / FALSE

5. Some pirates kept a parrot as a pet.
   TRUE / FALSE

6. The cook on a pirate ship was often a disabled sailor.
   TRUE / FALSE

7. Pirates were only interested in capturing treasure from the ships they attacked.
   TRUE / FALSE

8. 'Walking the plank' was the pirates' favourite way of disposing of their victims.
   TRUE / FALSE

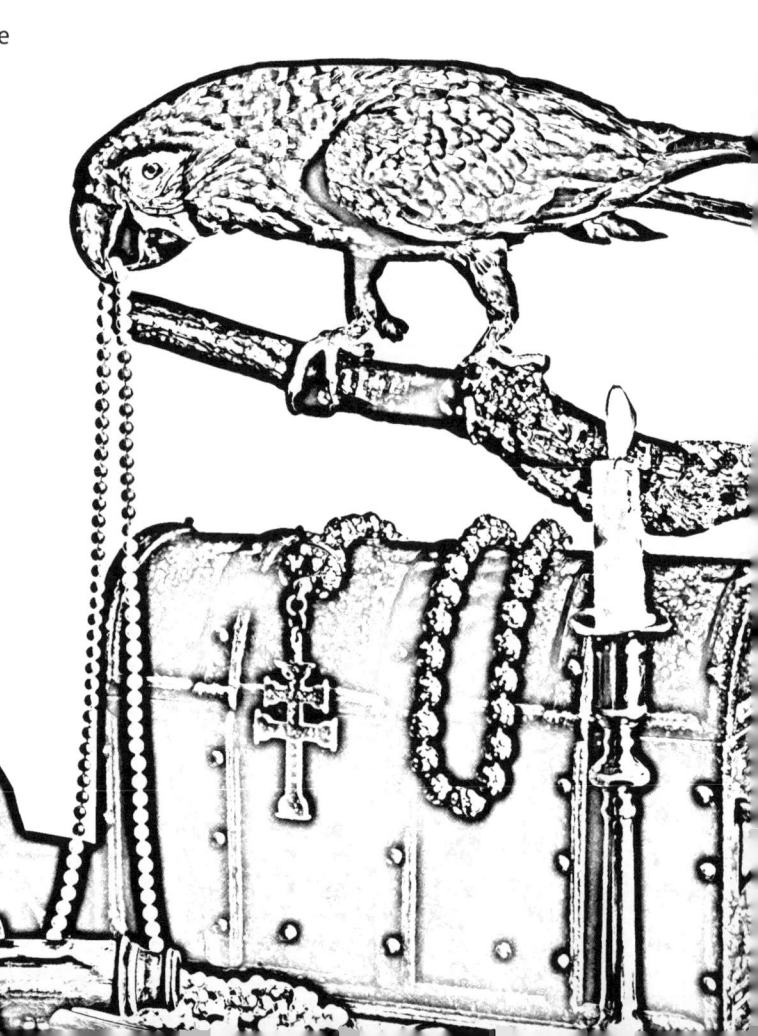

9. Pirates sailed in large ships which could carry many guns and overpower the opposition by strength and force.

    TRUE / FALSE

10. Pirate captains operated a code of conduct for their crews, also known as Articles of Regulation. Which of these rules would you expect to find in a pirate ship?

    (a) No gambling on board.
    (b) Lights out at 8.00 pm.
    (c) Anyone deserting their ship or leaving their battle-station will be killed or marooned.
    (d) No striking another man on board. All quarrels that cannot be resolved by reconciliation will be settled on land by duel, first with pistols; then, if there is no result, with cutlasses.
    (e) Musicians will have Sundays off.

11. When was the last public hanging of a pirate in Scotland?

    (a) 1705
    (b) 1725
    (c) 1822
    (d) 1881

12. Bartholomew Roberts, aka 'Black Bart', holds the record for the number of ships taken by a pirate. The number is believed to have been:

    (a) 60
    (b) 80
    (c) 120
    (d) 400

13. Pirate ships always flew a black flag with a skull and crossbones on it.

    TRUE / FALSE

14. Which Irish saint was, as a boy, captured by pirates?

    (a) St Adamnan
    (b) St Aidan
    (c) St Andrew
    (d) St Cuthbert
    (e) St Patrick

15. Which Scottish monarch, as heir to the throne, was captured by pirates?

    (a) William I, the Lion
    (b) Alexander III
    (c) James I
    (d) Mary Queen of Scots
    (e) James VI

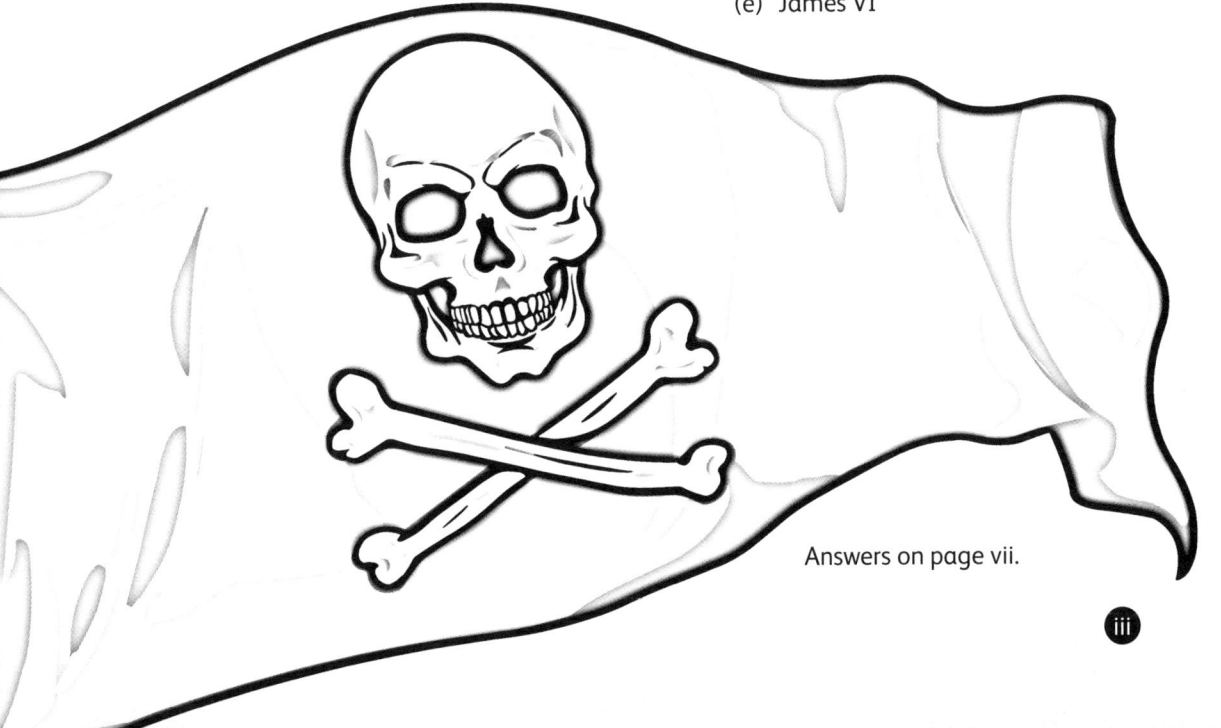

Answers on page vii.

Word search

Move diagonally, as well as up and down, in any direction, to find the following words:

Solution on page viii

BLACKBEARD
BOATSWAIN
BONNY
BOUNTY
CAPTAIN
DOLZELL
GALLEY
HIJACK
JOLLY ROGER
KIDD
LOWTHER
PARROT
PIECES OF EIGHT
PIRATE
PRIVATEER
READ
TREASURE
WOOD

I	D	H	S	N	Q	W	Z	J	M	E	E	O	J	W
K	C	A	J	I	H	O	G	G	N	B	C	W	O	Y
P	I	E	C	E	S	O	F	E	I	G	H	T	L	A
B	Z	T	V	I	W	D	W	R	B	T	Z	B	L	L
R	L	K	I	D	D	C	U	O	J	N	L	O	Y	C
V	E	A	R	E	E	T	A	V	I	R	P	U	R	R
K	E	A	C	K	L	T	O	A	A	G	H	N	O	A
E	P	R	D	K	S	O	T	R	A	C	Y	T	G	B
T	G	X	U	W	B	P	W	L	R	N	C	Y	E	Z
A	X	M	A	S	A	E	L	T	N	A	C	U	R	Z
R	Y	I	V	C	A	E	A	O	H	S	P	H	A	S
I	N	U	Y	M	Y	E	B	R	K	E	T	H	H	S
P	S	A	J	V	Q	R	R	G	D	X	R	R	E	G
T	V	S	U	Y	A	Y	Y	T	B	E	K	I	C	S
D	O	L	Z	E	L	L	Z	C	J	I	B	I	M	V

Pirate glossary

Members of the crew: In naval and merchant ships, more experienced members of the crew had special duties and names to go with them.

The **Master's** responsibility was to navigate the ship. The **Boatswain** looked after the sails, rigging and related gear.

The **Mate**, as in **Boatswain's Mate**, was the principal assistant. A **Mate** in the merchant navy, however, was an officer, **First Mate** being second only to the captain of the vessel.

Pirate: Someone who robs and plunders on or from the sea. Today it also means a person who steals someone's intellectual property, e.g. a design, artwork, musical composition, film, or a piece of writing.

There were different names for pirates in different parts of the world. **Corsairs** operated in the Mediterranean, especially off the Barbary Coast of north Africa. Pirates of the Caribbean and coast of South America were **buccaneers**.

Pirate ships: Pirates used different kinds of ship. A **galley** was a sailing ship whose sides were pierced for oars with which it could be propelled when there was no wind [see pages 2 and 7]. In the Mediterranean, this was a long, slim craft rowed by slaves.

A **galleon**, on the other hand, was a very large, heavily armed merchant vessel with several decks, principally used by the Spanish to transport treasure from South America.)

A **brig** or **brigantine** had two masts and mainly square sails, attached to horizontal poles called **yards** or **yardarms**. The most popular ship with pirates was a **sloop**, usually single-decked with one mast. The schooner had two masts. The sails of both sloop and schooner were set 'fore and aft', that is parallel to the ship's sides. They were hoisted out to catch the wind on horizontal struts (**booms** and **gaffs**) attached at one end to the masts on swivels.

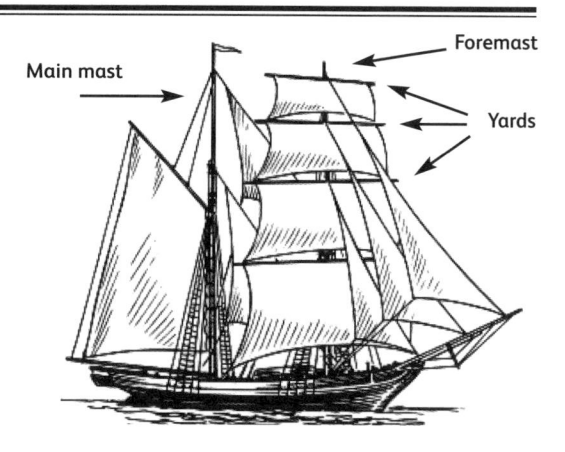

Privateer: The name given to an armed merchant vessel, or the captain or a member of the crew of such a vessel, which had been granted by its government a licence to attack, seize, or rob ships of a nation with which it was at war.

The licence itself was know as a **letter of marque**. By the 16th century it had become a cheap way of raising a navy without the expense of building new ships and maintaining their crews. A **letter of reprisal** was a licence issued in time of peace to enable a ship's owner or captain to gain satisfaction for a wrong that he claimed had been done to him at sea.

The value of any ships and their goods seized under licence was meant to be divided between the Crown and the owner, captain, and crew of the privateer – a similar system operated in the Royal Navy. Many privateers, however, used the licence as a cloak for piracy.

Pirate talk

Ahoy: a greeting; hello.
Batten down the hatches: get the ship ready for an upcoming storm.
Booty: pirate treasure.
Buccaneer: another name for a pirate.
Crow's nest: a place near the top of the main mast where a member of the crew can look out for other ships.
Cutlass: a pirate sword.
Davy Jones' Locker: the place where people go when drowned at sea.
Dead men tell no tales: the dead cannot betray any secrets.
Heave-ho: to pull on a rope as hard as possible.
Jolly Roger: the familiar pirate flag of the early 18th century, used by such individuals as Edward England, Black Sam Bellam and John Taylor. The flag has a white skull and crossbones beneath it, on a black background.
Landlubber: someone who is more at home on the land than the sea.
Man-of-War: a ship armed for combat from a legitimate (national) navy.

Pieces of eight: a common Spanish silver coin, worth eight *reales*, made famous by the parrot in Robert Louis Stevenson's novel, *Treasure Island* (see pages 19 and 37).
Powder monkey: an assistant to the gunner; often a young/small boy.
Scuttle: to sink a ship deliberately.
Sea-dog/Old salt: referring to an older member of the crew or someone who has been at sea for a long time.
Shiver me timbers: a sudden shock, such as an explosion or impact from another ship, causing the ship's timbers to vibrate.
Yo-ho-ho: a greeting; an expression of heartiness or good cheer.
Walking the plank: a form of punishment or execution by making the victim, with hands bound, walk along a plank set out over the sea from the ship's side – though this was rare among real pirates.
Weigh anchor: pull up the anchor and let's get going.

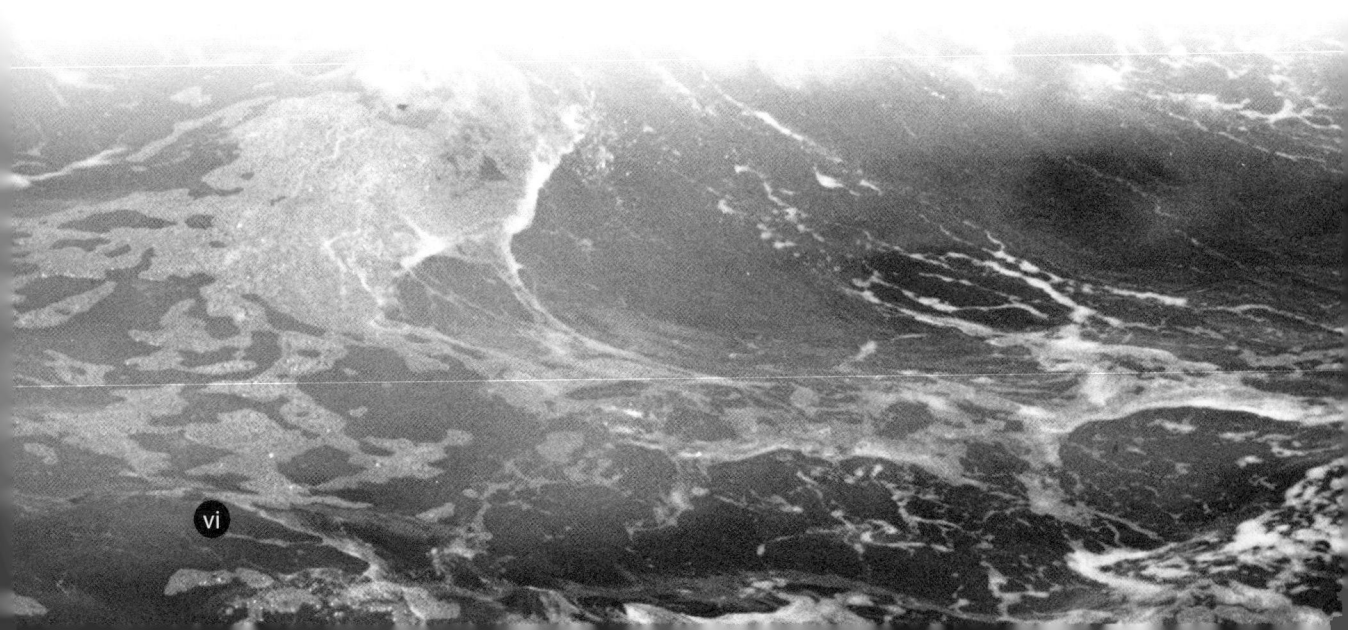

ANSWERS

PIRATES: TAKE THE TEST (pp. ii–iii)

1. **TRUE:** The Romans used the name *Scotti*, or *Scots*, for the Irish tribe of Dál Riata who first came to Scotland as raiders (see page 2).

2. **(a) FACT:** Captain Henry Avery (or Every) in 1694, as second mate of a privateer, organised a mutiny and took over the ship. Though his pirate career was brief, he made his fortune as commander of the flotilla of pirate ships which captured the treasure ship of the Great Mogul of India, *Ganj-i-Sawai*, in 1695.
   (b) FACT: Captain Edward 'Blackbeard' Teach operated as a pirate in the Bahamas and off the east coast of America from 1716 until his violent death two years later. Thinking he had overpowered two naval vessels sent to catch him, he boarded one, only to be ambushed by its crew. He was shot five times and took 20 deep slashes to the body before he died. His head was then cut off and hung from the bowsprit of the ship which captured him – as a warning to others.
   (c) and (d) FACT: Ann Bonny and Mary Read, posing as men, were among the fiercest members of the crew of Captain John Rackham (Calico Jack) who, with ten shipmates, was condemned to death in Jamaica in 1720. Bonny and Read were sentenced to be hanged. Both successfully appealed on the grounds of pregnancy. It is not known what happened to Bonny and her baby. Read died of fever in prison shortly after her trial.
   (e) FICTION: Captain Hook (see page 37) was described by author J. M. Barrie as being formerly Blackbeard's bosun.
   (f) FICTION: *The Pirates of Penzance* (1897) is a comic opera by W. S. Gilbert and Arthur Sullivan.
   (g) FICTION: Sir Ralph the Rover is the main character in 'The Inchcape Rock', a poem by Robert Southey.
   (h) FICTION: Long John Silver is the pirate chief, and dominant character, in Robert Louis Stevenson's adventure novel, *Treasure Island* (1883).

3. **(c)** Considering the difference in populations, 10% represents a high number when compared to the 35% of these pirates who were English born.

4. **TRUE:** Being a pirate was dangerous, not just from rough weather, but from injuries in battle which could cause the loss of a leg or arm. When there was no doctor on board, the ship's carpenter would be called upon to saw off the wounded part of the leg and replace it with one fashioned from wood. Sometimes the patient survived!

5. **TRUE:** Seamen often brought back birds and animals from their travels as pets. Parrots were popular as they could be taught to speak. One buccaneer captain reported, of a landing in the Bay of Campeche near Veracruz in 1676, that there was hardly a man in the ship who did not bring aboard one or two of the local parrots.

6. **TRUE:** Ships' cooks were usually seamen who had been disabled by accident or enemy action.

7. **TRUE:** Pirates were usually unable to return their ships to port for repairs, and for supplies of ropes and sails, and food and drink. Repairs were done at secret locations or at sea, and essential supplies looted from ships they attacked. These ships were also sources of fresh recruits to a pirate crew, either voluntarily or pressed. Sometimes pirates stole a whole ship, to replace or add to their fleet.

8. **FALSE:** Between the 17th and 19th centuries it was never a common practice to torture victims by blindfolding them, tying them up, and then forcing them into the sea to drown. Curiously, though, it was a favourite means by which pirates in Roman times disposed of people they did not like, especially Roman citizens. Important captives were held for ransom. Those of lesser status were made to put on their togas and official footwear, and then forced to climb down a rope ladder, rung by rung, into the sea.

9. **FALSE:** Pirate ships were usually small and fast, enabling them to be easier to manoeuvre and for their crews to make a quick getaway.

10. Astonishing though it may seem, *all* of these are rules which were commonly expected to be observed aboard a pirate ship.

11. 1822 (see page 9).

12. **(d)** Black Bart is reported to have taken 400 ships in his career as a pirate, which lasted just two years from 1720–22. He was killed in action against a naval ship off the coast of West Africa.

13. **FALSE:** The skull and crossbones on a black background was a principal means of frightening victims into submission without a fight. Known as the Jolly Roger, it is thought that this name was perhaps derived from the French *joli rouge* or 'pretty red', the colour of a French privateer's flag. Pirates flew a red flag to indicate that if there was any resistance, all prisoners would be slaughtered. They also carried several national flags, so that they could, at first sight, appear to be from a friendly country.

14. **(e)** St Patrick (see page 11).

15. **(d)** King James I (see pages 12–13).

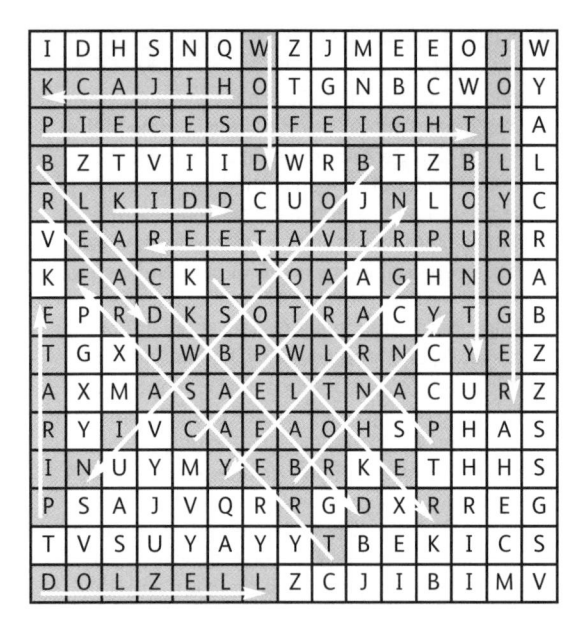

```
I D H S N Q W Z J M E E O J W
K C A J I H O T G N B C W O Y
P I E C E S O F E I G H T L A
B Z T V I I D W R B T Z B L L
R L K I D D C U O J N L O Y C
V E A R E E T A V I R P U R R
K E A C K L T O A G H N O A
E P R D K S O T R A C Y T G B
T G X U W B P W L R N C Y E Z
A X M A S A E L T N A C U R Z
R Y I V C A F A O H S P H A S
I N U Y M Y E B R K E T H H S
P S A J V Q R R G D X R R E G
T V S U Y A Y Y T B E K I C S
D O L Z E L L Z C J I B I M V
```

WORD SEARCH SOLUTION (page iv)

FURTHER CREDITS

Alamy Stock Photo /
2D Alan King – for page 30 (sea-battle A3WPN2); **Chronicle** – p. 11 (St Patrick G36J77); p. 23 (William Kidd G37MRA); **Granger Historical Picture Archive** – p. 9 (Sinking of the *Pandora* FF6ECW); p. 24 (Kidd striking Moore FFY2DK); p. 26 (hanging at Execution Dock FF72Y0); **North Wind Picture Archive** – p. 25 (hanging of Kidd A9YY95); **Photo 12** – p. 8 (Bligh taken from *Bounty* GG2GRW); **Pictorial Press Ltd** – p. 25 (Kidd before Commons CNYD9B); **The Picture Art Collection** – p. 13 (Bass Rock P5ND2B)

David Caldwell – p. 19 (Más a Tierra)

Crown Copyright HES – p. 5 (Kisimul Castle)

Eileen Kamm – p. 37 (Captain Cleveland); Activities, p. v (ship)

Library of Congress
p. 18 (cave, Más a Tierra 12858u); p. 21 (John Paul Jones 11545u); p. 31 (Edward Seegar 3b09545u); p. 32 (Visit of Cuna 3b16708u); p. 34 (3b09734u, 3b09735u – George Lowther, 'Ned' Low); p. 37 (*Treasure Island* 3b11003u); p. 38 (pirate justice 3b09550u)

Reproduced by permission of the National Library of Scotland – p. 18 (Robinson Crusoe); p. 27 (John Gow)

© National Maritime Museum, Greenwich, London – for p. 10 (ship's cook)

© National Museums Scotland (Library)
- Gosse, Philip 1924. *The Pirates Who's Who* (London, Dulau & Co. Ltd) – p. 28 (pressing a pirate)
- Navy Records Society, The 1912. *The Old Scots Navy 1249–1710*, vol. XLIV – p. 3 (carrack); p. 29 (Woods' victory); p. 35 (Captain Gordon)
- Rawson, Geoffrey 1930. *Bligh of the Bounty* (London, Philip Allan) – p. 7 (William Bligh)
- Hutchinson, J. R. 1913. *The Press-gang: Afloat and Ashore* (Eveleigh Nash) – p. 20 ('Manning the Navy')

www.SCRAN.ac.uk
Hunterian Museum & Art Gallery – p. 19 (pieces of eight); **Lennoxlove House Ltd** – p. 16 (Charles Stuart, 6th Duke of Lennox); **National Library of Scotland** – p. 13 (James I and Joan Beaufort); **© Newsquest (Herald & Times)** – p. 39 (*Mary Craig*, Invergordon Harbour); **University of Dundee** – p. 33 (surgical instruments)

shuttershock.com
Joe Benning – for p. 8 (Pitcairn 1206132022); **nikiteev_konstantin/shutterstock.com** – Activities, p. iii (flag, 188540999); **Pinehead Studio** – p. 7 (*liburna* 155760684); **Denis Simonov** – Activities, p. i (ship, 1177125682); **Triff** – for p. 1 (compass, 535317802)

© Western Isles Library – for p. 6 (original Stornoway Castle)

TITLES IN THE SCOTTIES SERIES
(editors: Frances and Gordon Jarvie)

The Clans (Gordon Jarvie)
The Covenanters (Claire Watts)
Flight in Scotland (Frances and Gordon Jarvie)
Greyfriars Bobby: A Tale of Victorian Edinburgh (Frances and Gordon Jarvie)
The Jacobites (Antony Kamm)
Mary, Queen of Scots (Elizabeth Douglas)
Robert Burns in Time and Place (Frances and Gordon Jarvie)
The Romans in Scotland (Frances Jarvie)
Scotland's Vikings (Frances and Gordon Jarvie)
Scottish Environments (Alan and Moira McKirdy)
Scottish Explorers (Antony Kamm)
Scottish Kings and Queens (Elizabeth Douglas)
Supernatural Scotland (Eileen Dunlop)
There shall be a Scottish Parliament (Frances and Gordon Jarvie)
Wallace and Bruce (Antony Kamm)